**Riffs, Chords & Tricks
you can learn today!**

# *Fast*Forward™
# Lead Guitar Solos

with Rikky Rooksby

**Wise Publications**
London / New York / Sydney / Paris / Copenhagen / Madrid

Exclusive Distributors:
**Music Sales Limited**
14/15 Berners Street, London W1T 3LJ, UK.
**Music Sales Pty Limited**
Units 3-4,17 Willfox Street, Condell Park, NSW 2200, Australia.
**Music Sales Corporation**
180 Madison Avenue, 24th floor, New York, NY10016, USA.

Order No. AM950939
ISBN 0-7119-7064-5
This book © Copyright 1998 by Wise Publications.

Book design by Michael Bell Design.
Edited and arranged by Rikky Rooksby.
Music processed by Barnes Music Engraving.
Cover photography by George Taylor.
Cover instrument kindly loaned by World Of Music.

Text photographs courtesy of London Features
International.

Printed in the United Kingdom.

Your Guarantee of Quality:
As publishers, we strive to produce every book to
the highest commercial standards.
The music has been freshly engraved and the book has
been carefully designed to minimise awkward page turns
and to make playing from it a real pleasure.
Particular care has been given to specifying acid-free,
neutral-sized paper made from pulps which have not
been elemental chlorine bleached.
This pulp is from farmed sustainable forests and
was produced with special regard for the environment.
Throughout, the printing and binding have
been planned to ensure a sturdy, attractive publication
which should give years of enjoyment.
If your copy fails to meet our high standards, please
inform us and we will gladly replace it.

www.musicsales.com

# Introduction

Hello, and welcome to ▶▶Fast*Forward*

Congratulations on purchasing a product that will improve your playing and provide you with hours of pleasure. All the music in this book has been specially created by professional musicians to give you maximum value and enjoyment.

If you already know how to 'drive' your instrument, but you'd like to do a little customising, you've pulled in at the right place. We'll put you on the fast track to playing the riffs and patterns that today's professionals rely on.

We'll provide you with a vocabulary of riffs that you can apply in a wide variety of musical situations, with a special emphasis on giving you the techniques that will help you in a band situation.

That's why the music examples in this book come with full-band audio tracks so that you get your chance to join in. All players and bands get their sounds and styles by drawing on the same basic building blocks. With ▶▶Fast*Forward* you'll learn these quickly, and then be ready to use them to create your own style.

# Playing A Solo

The singer turns away, the music surges, and the spotlight falls on the guitarist . . . light flashes off pick-up covers and a peal of notes ricochets around the concert hall – the guitar solo. You want to do that too – maybe you've already learned some scales, yet nothing seems to come together properly. This book will give you everything you need to start playing solos.

In this book you'll find many different examples of guitar solos. Most of them are quite short, clocking in at around 8, 12 or 16 bars, but the last example lasts for a full 40 bars. As you progress through the examples, you'll learn all the techniques you need to put together an authentic lead solo.

This book will give you ideas on scales, dynamics, and phrasing. You'll also learn how to begin and end a solo, how to use intervals, and a host of other tips. The music has been composed so that relative beginners and intermediate players will be able to progress throughout. If you are new to lead playing, I recommend that you also get a copy of *Lead Guitar Licks* in the ▶▶**Fast***Forward* series.

**Rikky Rooksby**

Each example is given in musical score and in guitar tablature. In tablature each number indicates the fret at which the note is played – each line represents a string. If you find it hard to remember which way up they go, always think of pitch: high notes are above low notes, therefore the high-sounding string (1st E) is at the top. Underneath the TAB you will find suggested left-hand fingerings (index = 1, middle = 2, ring = 3, little = 4). Other TAB symbols will be explained as we go along.

Each musical example is played once with the lead guitar, and once without. The first is for you to learn by listening, the second 'play-along' track is for you to practise.

The examples have a one-bar count-in.

 **TRACK 1: TUNING NOTES**

# The Best Kept Secret

Playing good solos depends on musical understanding. It's not only *what* you know, but knowing *how* to apply it. The first example will surprise you. The backing is an 8-bar break using what is known as a 'three chord trick' – the three major chords in the key of C major. Try playing the solo notated below over this backing - it uses the scale of C pentatonic major (C D E G A).

The pentatonic ('five-note') scale is the most common in rock and blues guitar. The solo starts on the lower strings and gradually works its way upward. Notice how the second four bars copy the first four – they use the same musical ideas but repeat them at a higher pitch. This idea of repetition at different octaves is an important technique.

TRACKS 2+3

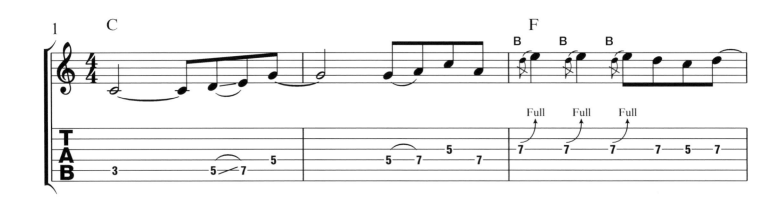

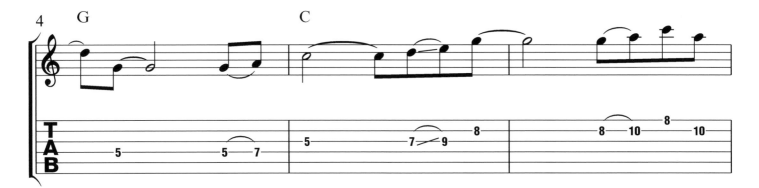

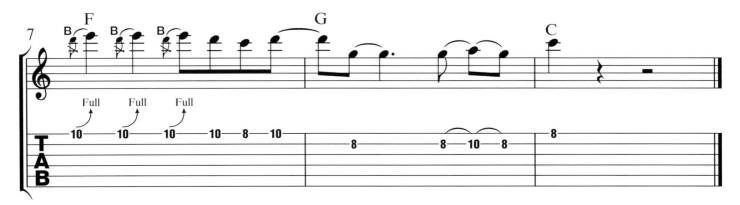

Now you're going to play *exactly* the same solo over another 8 bar break. This time you're in the key of A minor playing over the chords of Am, Dm and Em. It can't work, you say, surely the notes would have to change to fit these different chords? We must need another scale! Not so – try it. Hearing is believing!

TRACKS 4+5

You're playing the same notes as in the previous example, but they sound different – so what's going on?

Well, every major key has a 'relative minor' key associated with it; these two keys share the same notes. The relative minor key is always three frets below the major key. So A minor is the relative minor of C (i.e. it is 3 frets below C), D minor is the relative minor of F, and E is the relative minor of G. So, when you played over the chords of Am, Dm and Em you could use the same notes as you used when you played over the chords of C, F and G. The minor chords make the solo sound sad in comparison to the bright, upbeat mood of track 2.

The scale you used in the first example was called C pentatonic major – its equivalent in A minor is called A pentatonic minor. Its notes are A C D E G. Compare them with the notes of C pentatonic major – C D E G A. The two scales are the same notes arranged in a different order. That's why it worked!

Congratulations. You have just learned two important concepts about lead guitar solos:

1. Every pentatonic scale is at once a major *and* a minor. It is the backing harmony that decides which it sounds like.

2. The musical value of the notes you play is largely decided by the chords you are playing over.

Remember these ideas. For example, point 2 means that every single idea, phrase or scale that you know will sound different in different musical situations. That's why it's essential to know *how* to apply what you learn.

# Scales – The Tools Of The Trade

Although there are many types of scale, the majority of rock solos are performed using very few. Don't worry that you've got to learn 36 scales in 12 positions, all over the fretboard, before you can play a half-decent solo. All the solos in this book will be played with the scales described below.

Here's the scale of A pentatonic minor with the root note on the 6th string. This was the scale you used when you played along with track 5.

**TRACK 6**

Now try the same scale with a slight change of position that will allow you to go a little higher up the neck. I call the last six notes of this the 'extension box'.

**TRACK 7**

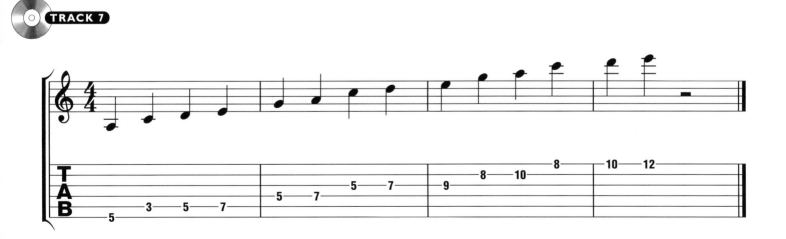

This is a different version of A pentatonic minor starting with the root note A on the 5th string.

This sounds an octave higher than the previous two scales (this is indicated above the music by the *8va* sign).

 TRACK 8

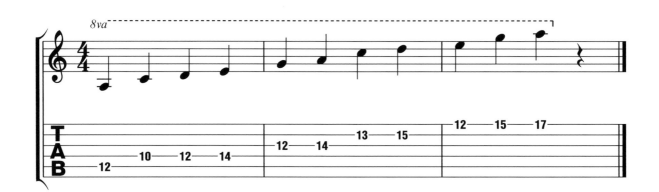

Here's a new scale – A pentatonic major, which starts with the root note on the 6th string.

 TRACK 9

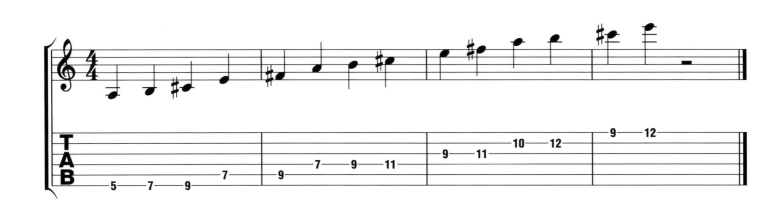

You can also add an 'extension box' to
A pentatonic major, which will allow you to play
a little higher up the neck.

TRACK 10

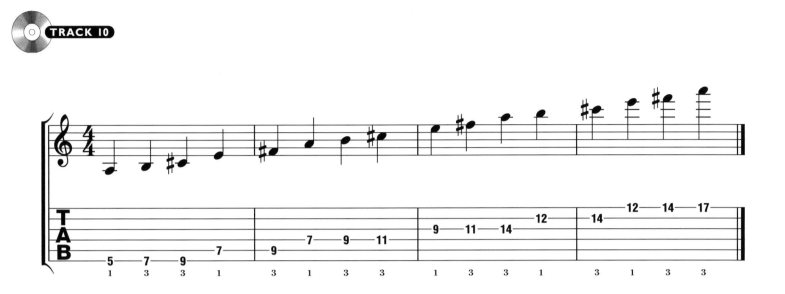

Here is the same scale starting with the root
note A on the 5th string. Once again, the
*8va* sign indicates that this scale sounds an
octave higher.

TRACK 11

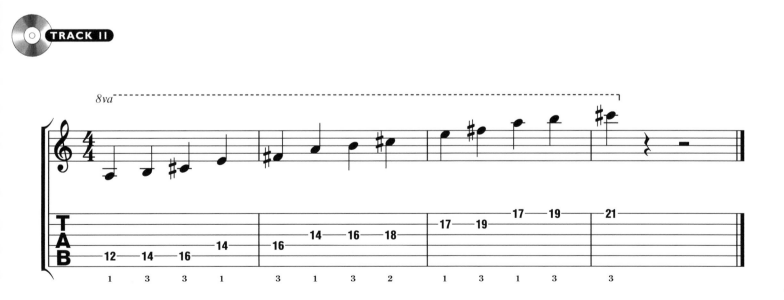

Another new scale – this one is called A natural minor. It has 7 notes in contrast to the pentatonic's five. If you compare them – A B C D E F G with A C D E G – you'll see that the pentatonic minor is a sort of 'edited' version of the natural minor.

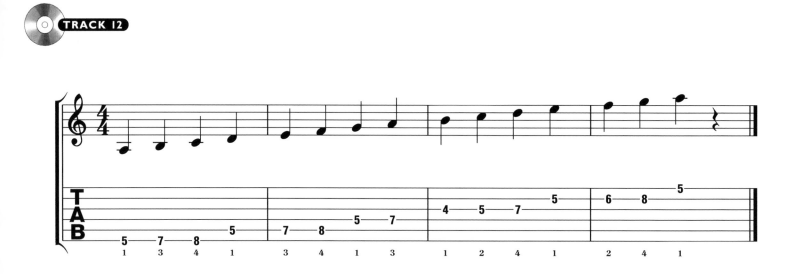

This is another version of A natural minor starting with the root note A on the 5th string.

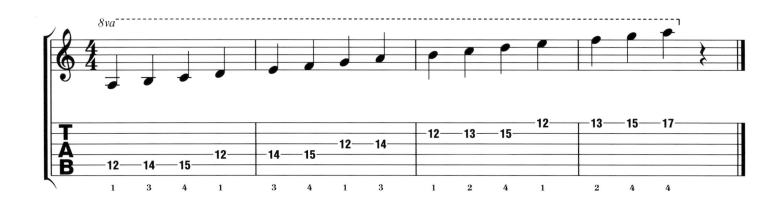

Here's the scale of A major with the root note on the 6th string. Again, this scale has 7 notes in contrast to the pentatonic's five. If you compare them – A B C♯ D E F♯ G♯ with A B C♯ E F♯ –

you'll see that, just as the pentatonic minor is an 'edited' version of the natural minor, the pentatonic major is an 'edited' version of the major scale.

**TRACK 14**

This is A major one octave higher, with the root note on the 5th string.

**TRACK 15**

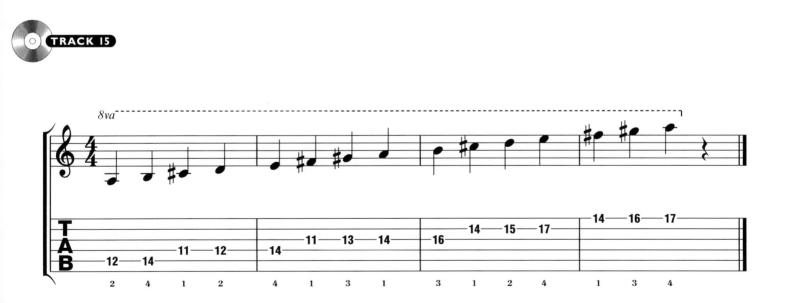

▶▶ **KEITH RICHARDS**
*"I look at that guitar sounding and think, there's only six strings and twelve frets, man. But the more you play it, the more things come out of it."*

Notice that none of the patterns above have any open strings in them. This means that they are *movable*. If you need to play in a different key, you simply select the right scale for the key and move the pattern up or down until the starting note is the same as the key note.

For example, if you wanted to play in the key of D minor you could take the A pentatonic minor scale that starts on the 6th string 5th fret and move it up to the 10th fret which is D. Alternatively, if you took the A pentatonic pattern whose root note is on the 5th string 12th fret and moved it down to the 5th fret, which is the note D, you'd also have a correct pattern. As long as you play the pattern correctly in the new position all the notes will come out properly in the new key.

The patterns above will allow you to play scales with their root notes on either the 6th or 5th string. This gives you at least two places on the neck to play any given scale, one higher or lower than the other.

Remember also that there are certain magic numbers that open up the fretboard. One of them is 12 – if you move a pattern up or down the neck 12 frets (provided that you don't fall off either end), the scale will have moved an octave higher or lower. So the A pentatonic minor scale at the 5th fret moved up twelve frets to the 17th fret consists of the same notes an octave higher.

Use these patterns to warm up your hands before playing the guitar. Played regularly with a metronome they can help you to build up your speed. Increase the speed of the metronome slowly as you get used to a given rate of notes per beat.

Congratulations again! You have now learnt a major, a natural minor, a pentatonic major and a pentatonic minor scale pattern – and you can play each of them in two positions, starting either on the 5th or the 6th strings. That's 8 patterns, which can be moved up and down each of the twelve frets in an octave, to give you a total of 96 scales! It wasn't that painful, was it?

Now we can put them to use – to make a scale sound like a solo it has to be phrased . . .

# The Heart Of Rock 'n' Roll
## Four Pentatonic Solos

Here's an 8-bar break using the A pentatonic minor scale over an A major backing. Normally you can't play a minor scale in a major key, but in blues-based rock the chord sequences allow this – the ear accepts the slight 'clash' as the tough quality of the rock sound. Notice the repetition of the first phrase an octave higher in bar 2 and the 'extension box' phrase in bar 7.

TRACKS 16+17

Using the same 8-bar backing in A major, let's play a break which uses alternate pentatonic major and minor scales to add variety. It has 4 clearly defined phrases and starts on the lower strings and works its way upward. The third phrase's major sound is balanced by the bluesier pentatonic minor phrase that follows it.

TRACKS 18+19

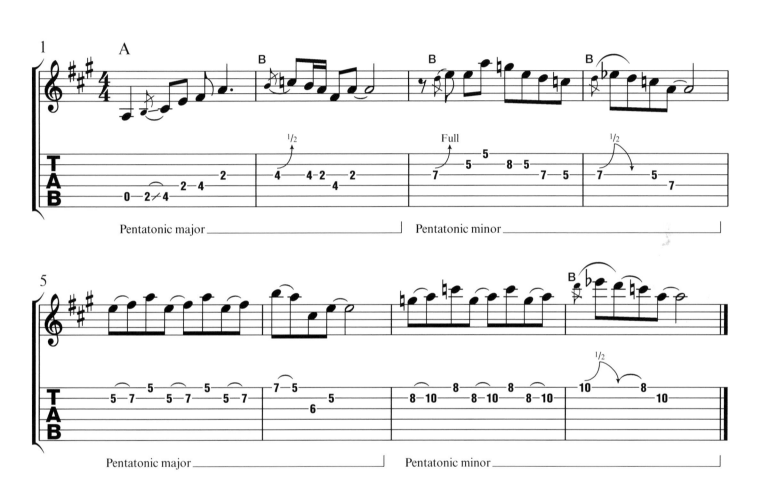

Now let's add another chord to create a two-chord sequence. Although you're still using the same scale (A pentatonic minor), when you play it over the D chord it sounds different, as we saw in the very first solo you learned. As the backing changes to D at bar 3, you are hitting the note D (7th fret on the 3rd string) – that's why that note sounds so fitting. Going to the root note of the chord over which you're playing always has this strong effect, especially on a change.

In bar 4, prepare for the first three notes by using your first finger to bar the top two strings at the 5th fret. Bend the G string with your third finger and release the note from the fretboard as soon as it's played so it 'runs' into the two above it. The high repeated bend in bar 8 finishes off the break with a sense of drama.

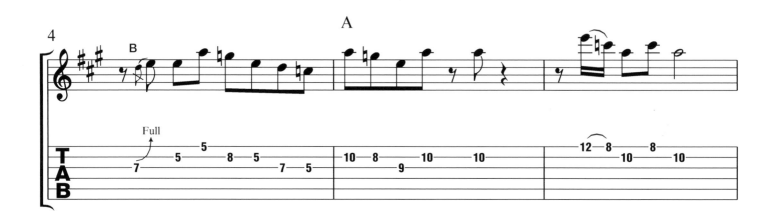

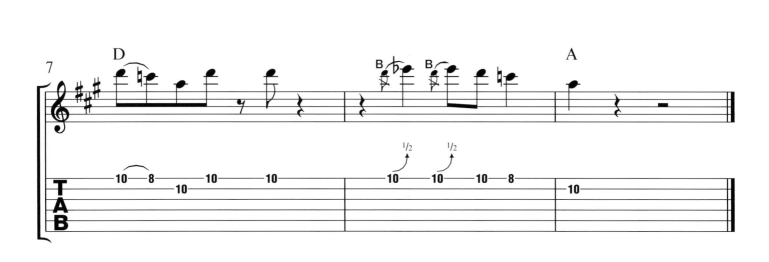

The backing track now contains a third chord, E major, so we have a 'three-chord trick' in A major. The inclusion of this chord will give you new opportunities.

This four-phrase break is built around a small cluster of notes at the 10th fret – showing that you don't have to wander all over the neck. Notice the increased use of bends – this allows you to use other notes without moving your hand position on the neck.

Phrases 1 and 3 are similar but not identical to each other – this gives the solo a feeling of consistency and unity, but ensures that it remains interesting. *Repetition with variation* is a good rule for solos. The overall feel of this solo is major but note the C natural in bar 3 (a 'blues note' from the pentatonic minor), which adds contrast.

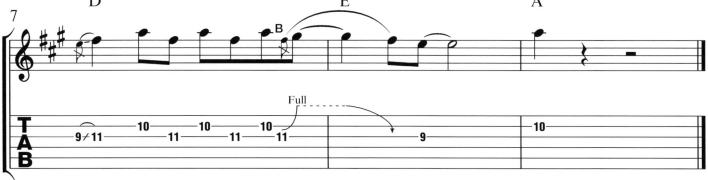

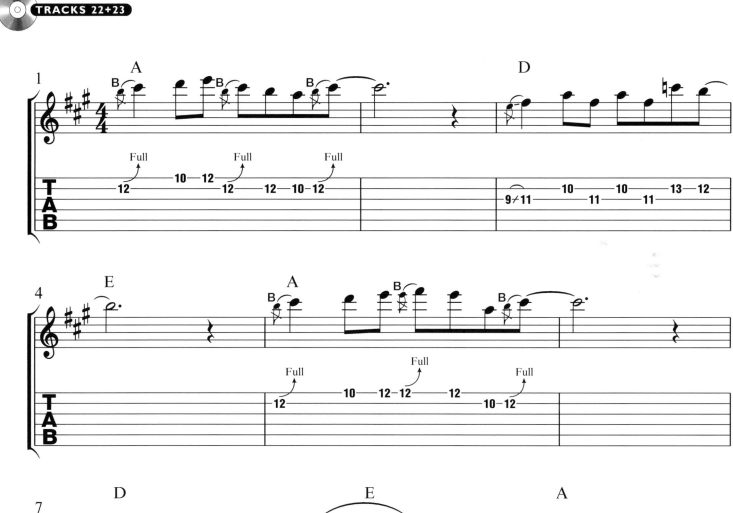

# If It Ain't Got Swing, It Ain't Worth A Thang

The most neglected aspect of playing good lead
solos is *rhythm*. Players often worry about how
many scales they know, or if they're playing the
right notes – but they don't ask themselves,
"Is my solo playing interesting rhythmically?".

This is one of the trickiest aspects of lead soloing
– everyone develops their own personal,
'signature' rhythms. It's not as if there are right
and wrong ways of doing it. A good rule for
relative beginners to remember is: what ever you
play, play it with rhythmic conviction so it sounds
as though you know exactly where you are
putting your notes in relation to the beat. A
simple phrase played with conviction will sound
better than a complicated phrase played out of
time.

You'll find the rhythm of the backing greatly
influences the rhythm of your solo. For example,
try this 12-bar break with a definite swing
rhythm. The slight 50s influence is reflected in
the double-notes at the start of the solo, which
derive from a style popularized by Chuck Berry.
Notice how the lead guitar 'hugs' the *rhythm* of
the track.

Lead solos don't always have to be about scales
and single notes. You can also play more than
one note at a time, or use chord shapes to
generate 'arpeggios' – the notes of a chord played
one after the other. Another technique used here
is the scale that doubles back on itself in bar 10 –
this allows you to get more notes out of the scale
pattern. The solo ends high up at the 17th fret
with a sequence of classic rock'n'roll notes and a
high bend.

**► PAUL WELLER**
"If someone plays a brilliant solo I don't know whether it's good or bad,
the only criteria I've got is if it sounds any good to me."

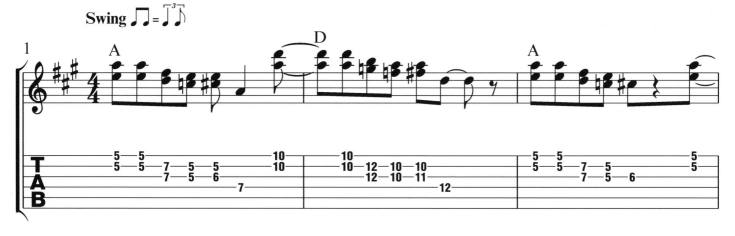

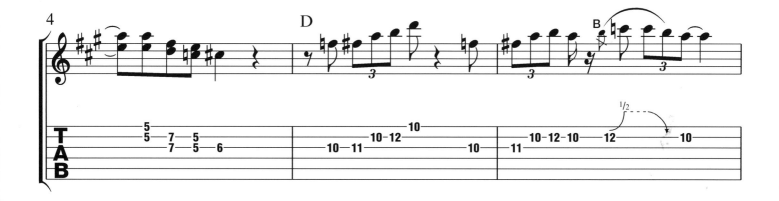

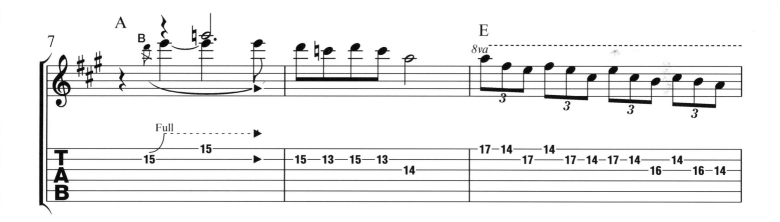

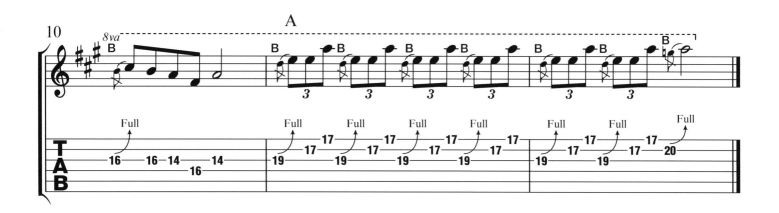

# Room With A View – Using Space

From the previous example you can see that a lead guitarist needs to be harmonically and rhythmically aware. Of course, you need to know your scales and the chords you're playing over, but you must also think about the rhythm of the music, its tempo, and whether it has moments of space that you can take advantage of. Here are two 16-bar breaks that have definite rhythmic patterns you can exploit to good effect.

In the first the chords alternate between A and D for four bars, before the rhythm guitar becomes fuller and moves onto the chords of E, C, and D. Note that, although these are major chords, they are also the notes of A pentatonic minor

(A C D E G). In the first 4 bars the lead guitar plays short phrases, which fill in the gaps left by the chord stabs in the backing, then moves into two ascending phrases which are similar but end differently.

In bars 9-12 you'll notice the use of a 'unison bend'. This is a way of producing the same note on adjacent strings and has the effect of emphasising that note. In bars 13-16 the same technique is used, but the notes are played one after the other – this is called a 'sequential unison bend'. The emphasis is strongly on the A pentatonic minor scale.

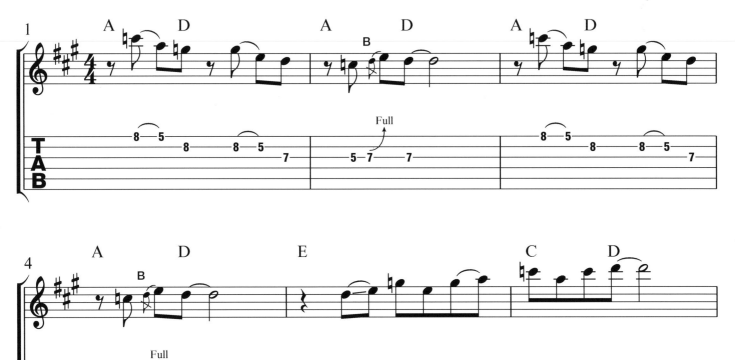

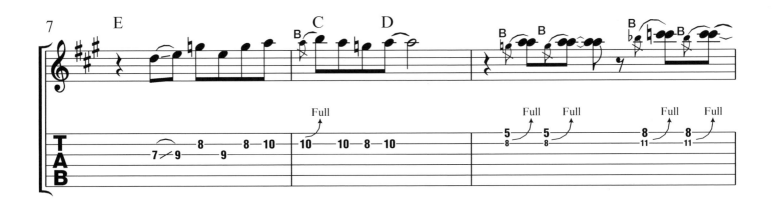

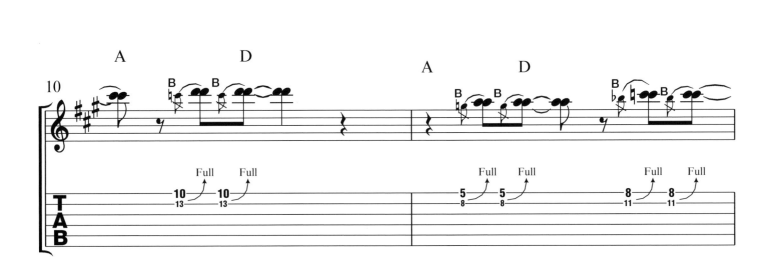

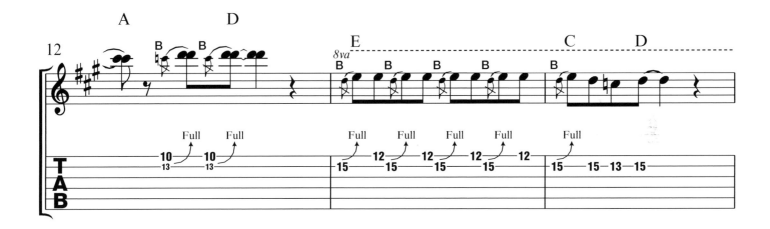

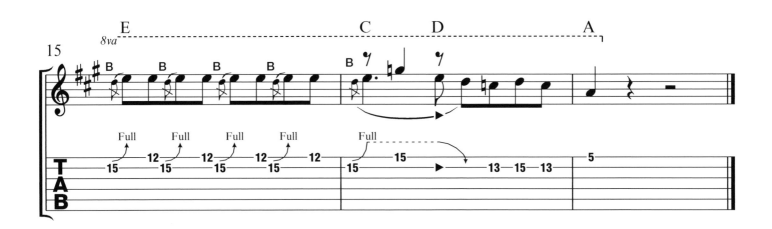

"I don't even remember the guitar solo on 'Teen Spirit'. It would take me five minutes to sit in the catering room and learn the solo."

In the next example the key is E major. In the first 8 bars, there are some long gaps before the backing really kicks in. The first high bent E is a sudden beginning, thrown into this space. It's held – which creates expectation for what comes next – before falling into several phrases on an E pentatonic minor scale at the 12th fret (root note on 6th string). Notice how the cut-offs in the solo accentuate the space in the music. In bar 9 we have some more distinctive Chuck Berry double-note chords contrasted with single-note phrases. A high bend gives a traditional finish.

▶▶ SANTANA
"I'm trying to sing through my guitar. I want my guitar to be more like a voice. People are interested in listening to the guitar that way."

# Long Lines For Long Days

Time to chill out for a second after all this uptight rock'n'roll. The next example is a dreamy, relaxed sequence in D major, but the combination of major 7 and minor chords means that playing D pentatonic minor will sound horrendous. If you don't believe me, try it over the backing track. For this style of music you need to use D pentatonic major or D major. The melody given here uses all the notes of D major. There are no bends to speak of – instead, we're going to phrase in long melodic lines and put in a few slides for expression.

**TRACKS 30+31**

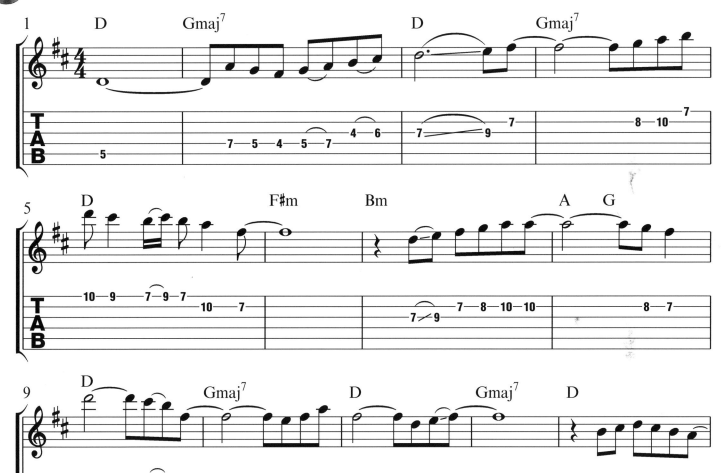

Now try this typically Britpop 16-bar sequence in D major – it's got a couple of blues chords thrown in just to keep you on your toes! Look out for the F chord in bars 4 and 12, and the C in bars 5 and 13. The D pentatonic major scale will sound fine, except on these chords, so the solo has been carefully adjusted at these points.

In bar 4 E is bent just a semitone to F, instead of the more usual F♯, and a D pentatonic

minor is then used over the C chord (its notes are D F G A C). Bars 9-10 use a complete D pentatonic major with the root on the 5th string – then comes a fast hammer-on phrase at the 10th fret for the D chord which moves down two frets for the F chord and then onto the next two strings for the C. This kind of movement is satisfying to the ear because it's so harmonically locked-in with the backing. Another couple of 'double-stops' bring the solo to a conclusion.

TRACKS 32+33

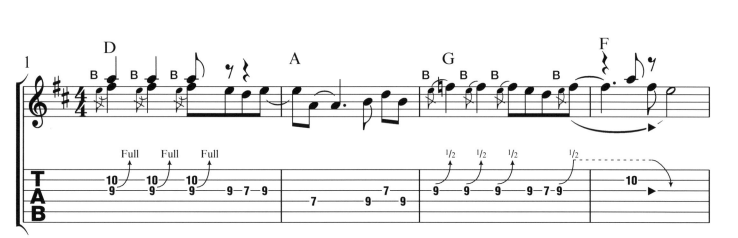

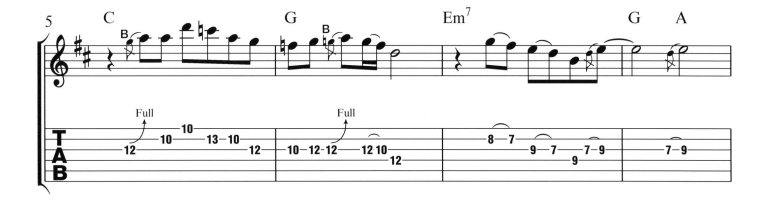

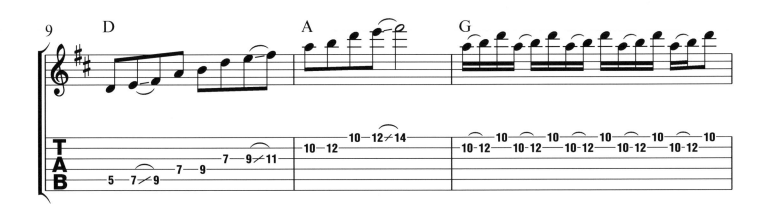

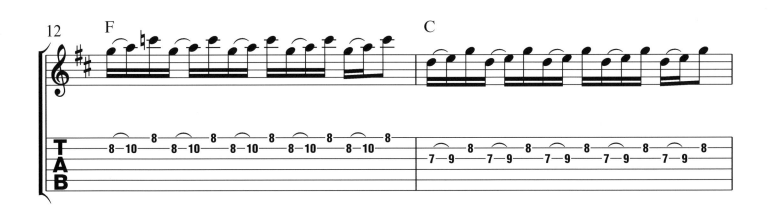

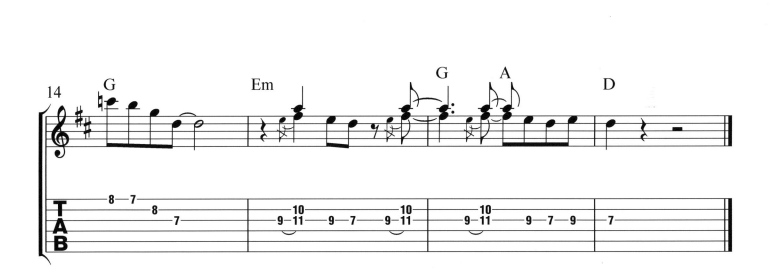

# Wot? No Harmony? – The Rock Trio

So far, all the backing tracks you have played
solos over have had two rhythm guitars playing
chords, so there was no doubt about the
harmony. They have been spelling out the major
and minor tonality of the changes. But what
happens if you're in a trio of drums, bass, guitar
and have no second guitar or keyboard? You have
to be rhythm and lead guitarist in one. When
you take a solo, there are suddenly no chords!
The resulting space can sound empty unless you
handle it properly.

You could simply play long phrases or cram as
many notes as you can into the gap. However,
there are other, more subtle ways; one method is
to play more 'double-stops', so that as you play
the melody, you are also sketching out the
harmony. This means using arpeggios and
double-stops based on the notes of the chords of
the sequence.

In the first example the neutral bass-drums
backing is turned into A major by implying the
chords that would be found in that key. Notice
the arpeggios moving up and down in the first
four bars, the double-stops in the next few bars
(ascending and descending) and in bars 9-10.
The solo finishes with single notes in bars 11-12.

# ▶▶ FastForward™
# Guide To Guitar

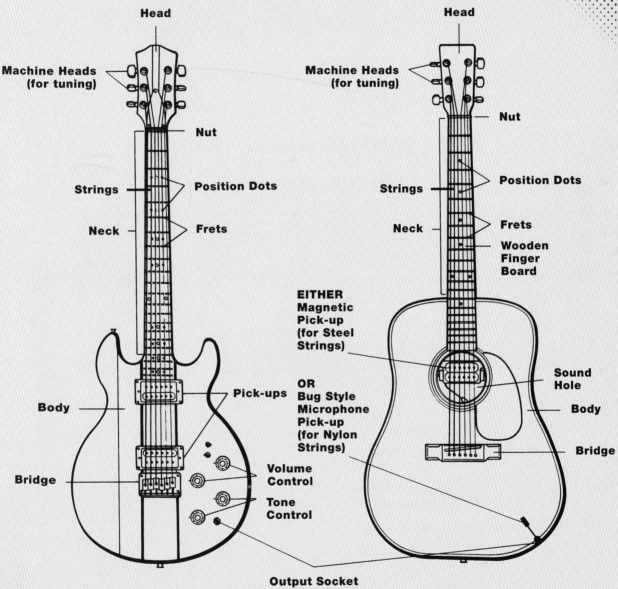

Head

Machine Heads
(for tuning)

Nut

Strings

Position Dots

Neck

Frets

Body

Pick-ups

Bridge

Volume
Control

Tone
Control

Output Socket
(to audio amplifier)

Head

Machine Heads
(for tuning)

Nut

Strings

Position Dots

Neck

Frets

Wooden
Finger
Board

EITHER
Magnetic
Pick-up
(for Steel
Strings)

OR
Bug Style
Microphone
Pick-up
(for Nylon
Strings)

Sound
Hole

Body

Bridge

### The Guitar

Whether you have an acoustic or an electric guitar, the principles of playing are fundamentally the same, and so are most of the features on both instruments.

In order to 'electrify' an acoustic guitar (as in the diagram), a magnetic pick up can be attached to those guitars with steel strings or a 'bug' style microphone pick-up can be attached to guitars with nylon strings.

If in doubt check with your local music shop.

# Tuning Your Guitar

### Tuning
Accurate tuning of the guitar is essential, and is achieved by winding the machine heads up or down. It is always better to 'tune up' to the correct pitch rather than down.

Therefore, if you find that the pitch of your string is higher (sharper) than the correct pitch, you should 'wind down' below the correct pitch, and then 'tune up' to it.

### Relative Tuning
Tuning the guitar to itself without the aid of a pitch pipe or other tuning device.

### Other Methods Of Tuning
Pitch pipe
Tuning fork
Dedicated electronic guitar tuner

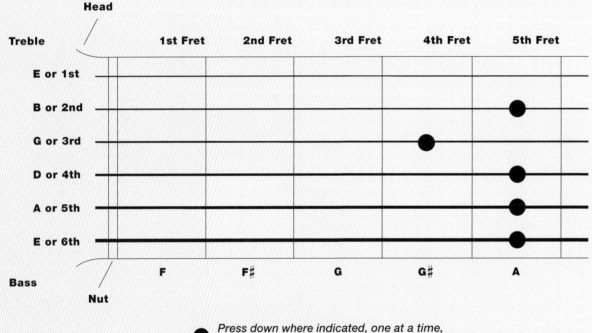

● Press down where indicated, one at a time, following the instructions below.

Estimate the pitch of the 6th string as near as possible to **E** or at least a comfortable pitch (not too high or you might break other strings in tuning up).

Then, while checking the various positions on the above diagram, place a finger from your left hand on:

- The 5th fret of the E or 6th string and **tune the open A** (or 5th string) to the note (A)

- The 5th fret of the A or 5th string and **tune the open D** (or 4th string) to the note (D)

- The 5th fret of the D or 4th string and **tune the open G** (or 3rd string) to the note (G)

- The 4th fret of the G or 3rd string and **tune the open B** (or 2nd string) to the note (B)

- The 5th fret of the B or 2nd string and **tune the open E** (or 1st string) to the note (E)

# Chord Boxes

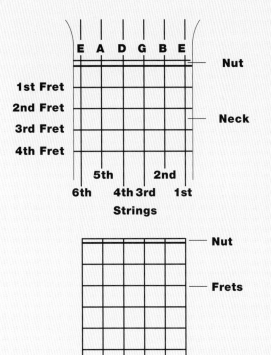

E A D G B E
Nut
1st Fret
2nd Fret
3rd Fret
4th Fret
Neck
5th  2nd
6th  4th 3rd  1st
**Strings**

Nut
Frets
**Strings**

### The A Chord

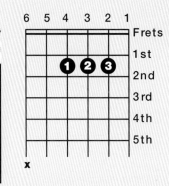

6 5 4 3 2 1
Frets
1st
❶ ❷ ❸
2nd
3rd
4th
5th
x

**x** = do not play this string

All chords are major chords unless otherwise indicated.

Chord boxes are diagrams of the guitar neck viewed head upwards, face on, as illustrated in the above drawings. The horizontal double line at the top is the nut, the other horizontal lines are the frets. The vertical lines are the strings starting from E or 6th on the left to E or 1st on the right.

Any dots with numbers inside them simply indicate which finger goes where. Any strings marked with an **x** must not be played.

The fingers of your hand are numbered 1, 2, 3, & 4 as in the diagram below.

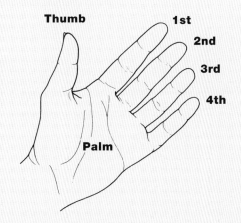

Thumb        1st
             2nd
             3rd
             4th
Palm

### Left Hand
Place all three fingers into position and press down firmly. Keep your thumb around the middle of the back of the neck and directly behind your 1st and 2nd fingers.

### Right Hand Thumb Or Plectrum
Slowly play each string, starting with the 5th or A string and moving up to the 1st or E string.

*If there is any buzzing, perhaps you need to:-*
Position your fingers nearer the metal fret (towards you); or adjust the angle of your hand; or check that the buzz is not elsewhere on the guitar by playing the open strings in the same manner.

*Finally*, your nails may be too long, in which case you are pressing down at an extreme angle and therefore not firmly enough. Also the pad of one of your fingers may be in the way of the next string for the same reason.

So, cut your nails to a more comfortable length and then try to keep them as near vertical to the fretboard as possible.

Once you have a 'buzz-free' sound, play the chord a few times and then remove your fingers and repeat the exercise until your positioning is right instinctively.

# Holding The Guitar

The picture above shows a comfortable position for playing rock or pop guitar

### The Right Hand
When STRUMMING (brushing your fingers across the strings), hold your fingers together.

When PICKING (plucking strings individually), hold your wrist further away from the strings than for strumming.

Keep your thumb slightly to the left of your fingers which should be above the three treble strings as shown.

### The Plectrum
Many modern guitar players prefer to use a plectrum to strike the strings. Plectrums come in many sizes, shapes and thicknesses and are available from your local music shop.

Start with a fairly large, soft one if possible, with a grip. The photo shows the correct way to hold your plectrum.

### The Left Hand
Use your fingertips to press down on the strings in the positions described. Your thumb should be behind your 1st and 2nd fingers pressing on the middle of the back of the neck.

RM 92051B

**Pull-Out Chart**

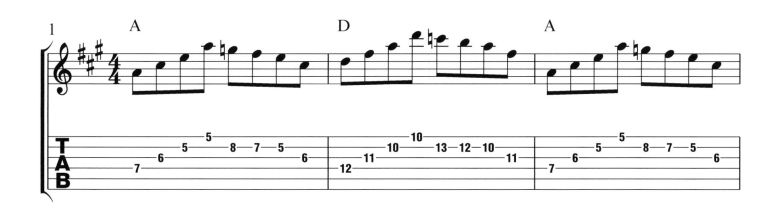

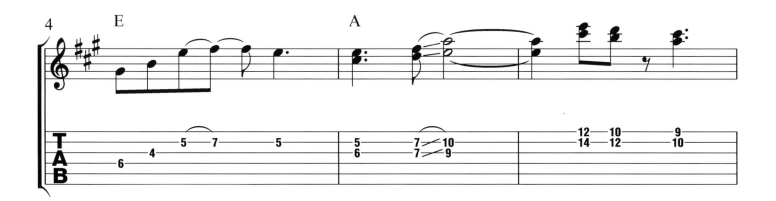

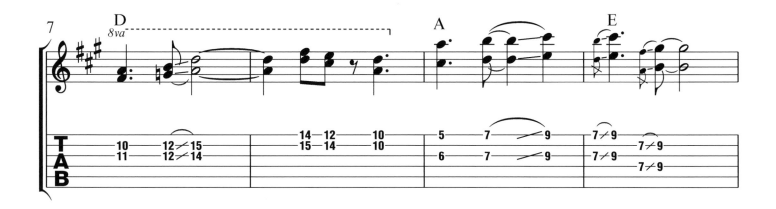

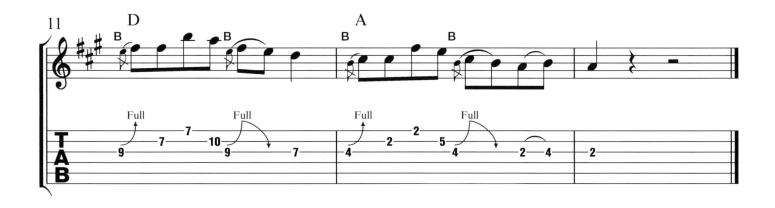

Next, let's take exactly the same backing and turn it into an A minor progression by using the appropriate double-stops and arpeggios.

In bars 5-8 you'll hear one very useful technique which is possible in certain keys: the playing of an open string which is in key at the same time as a fretted string. In bar 5, the open top E sounds below the fretted notes, then in bar 7 the open fourth string combines with the fretted note to imply D minor. The solo finishes with phrases based on E minor 7, D minor 7 and finally A minor 9 arpeggios.

**TRACKS 36+37**

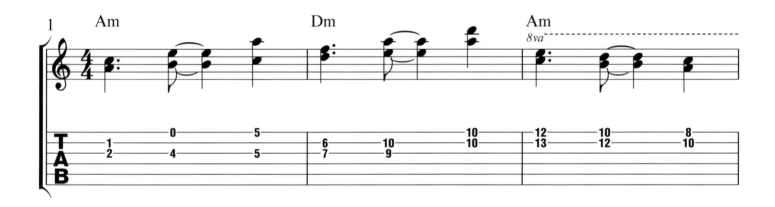

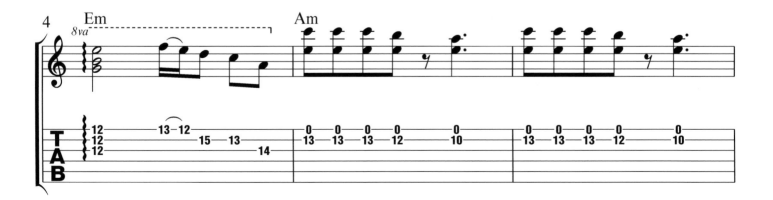

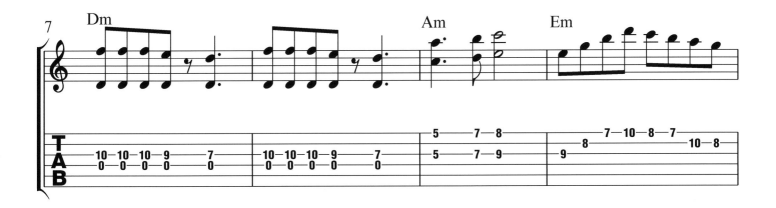

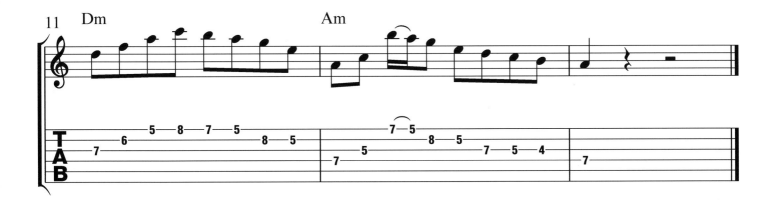

The important thing to remember about these two examples is that the *harmony was generated entirely by the guitar.* The bass did not play a single note that might have told you whether the chords were major or minor. You made it one, and then the other by your choice of notes.

▶▶ **THE EDGE**

"I use a lot of harmonised strings, even in my solos - like droning, say, the E string against something I was doing on the B string. I don't play proper guitar."

# Two Major Chord Sequences

Here's a 16 bar sequence in E major, using E, A, B, and D chords. There are two contrasting lead breaks.

In the first we start with an E pentatonic major scale around the 9th fret which is played in triplets, giving a bouncy feel. The scale uses the 'doubling back' technique which we looked at earlier to produce more notes from the scale.

In bars 3-4 the same idea is repeated but notice that one note has been changed – G♯ on the 2nd string has become an A to make it sit better with the A chord over which it is being played. Then come two 'double-stop' ideas for the D and B chords and in bars 7-8 a phrase which locks in to the rhythm of the backing and reinforces the A to E chord change.

Notice the double-stops in bars 9-10 – these octaves are repeated in 11-12, but as in bars 3-4, the A is substituted for G♯ to match the different chord. In bars 13-14 ascending double-stops are used over the D and B chords, and the solo rounds off with a 12th fret phrase. Notice how the change from G to G♯ over the last barline gives a distinctive effect – this is due to the mixing of the pentatonic major and the pentatonic minor.

*"Over the years I've come to look at solos more as little pieces within the song. You can make the solo fit the overall picture better. On the first record it was like, "All right! I get to solo!" and I'd blaze without thinking."*

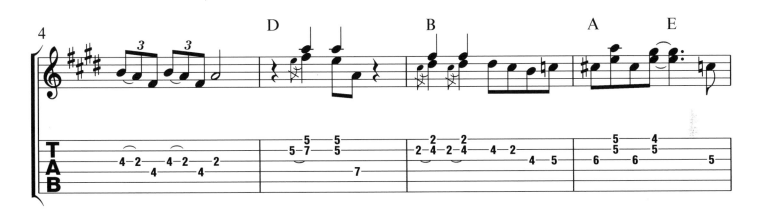

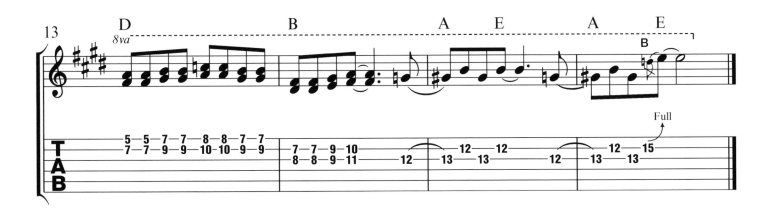

Now let's try a different approach to the same sequence.

This solo starts with the E pentatonic major scale, using a distinctive bend low down on the bottom string. This idea is then repeated on A using an A pentatonic major pattern whose root note also starts on the bottom string.

At bar 5 the solo shifts to a D pentatonic major scale (root on the 5th string), and then changes to a B pentatonic major in bar 6. The 4 notes in this bar correspond to the 'extension box' for a B pentatonic major scale starting at the 2nd fret of the 5th string.

The first half of the sequence ends with a descending E pentatonic major scale which walks right across the backing rhythm. Notice the chromatic B♭ at the end of bar 8 – this leads us down to an E pentatonic minor scale with the same bend as bar 1 but an octave higher (remember, *repetition with variation!*).

This idea is then repeated in bars 11-12 on an A pentatonic minor scale – so bars 9-12 re-state the first four bars in a minor scale. This solo ends with a high bend and then a two octave drop down to the bottom E string – contrasting phrases on varying octaves is a good way of breaking up the gradual rising / falling of scale-pattern movement.

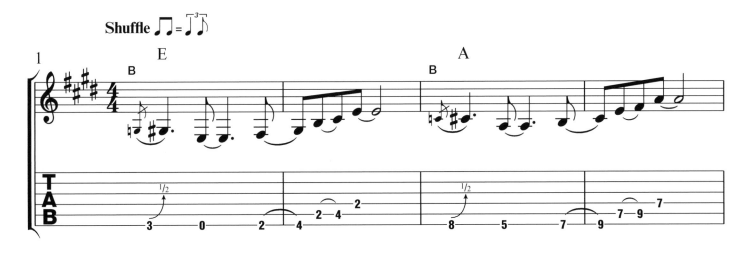

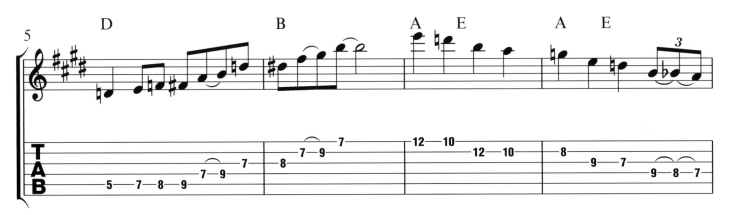

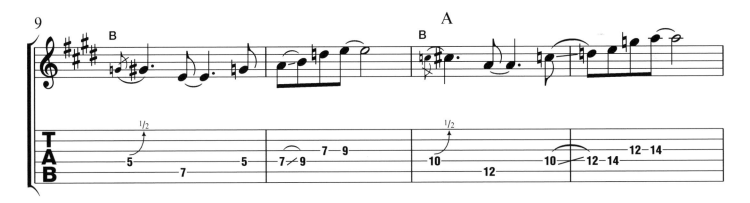

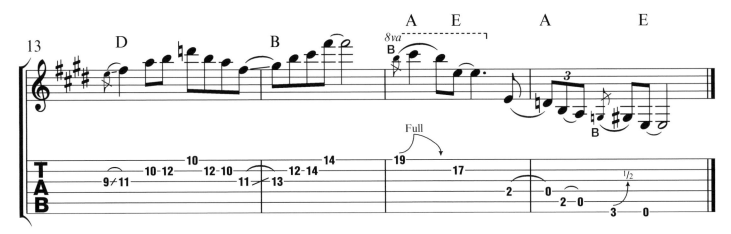

▶▶ *MARK KNOPFLER*
    *"I just steal a lick or two and use it my own way. That's all guitar players do,
    I think, they just steal licks off each other and then make it their own somehow."*

# Two Minor Chord Sequences

Having tried two solos over a major backing, let's now try soloing over a much slower minor-sounding sequence. The following examples are in E minor, so the main scales that are useful are E natural minor and E pentatonic minor.

The first solo is deliberately constructed in a reserved mood – in other words, although it is possible to play an aggressive, extrovert solo over these chords, this first example opts instead to hold back. The idea is to draw the listener *into* the music. Notice the use of long sustained notes and the effect of leaving gaps in the lead – never feel that you must play all the time in a solo.

The second half of the solo repeats the B-D-B motif first heard in bar 3, but plays it muted – put the edge of your picking hand on the strings near the bridge to muffle the strings a little. This phrase recurs three times, and in each case is followed by an answering phrase. Notice also the distinctive semitone bend from B to C against the A minor chord in the last two bars.

"*For big bends I use all three fingers - my ring backed by the index and middle.*"

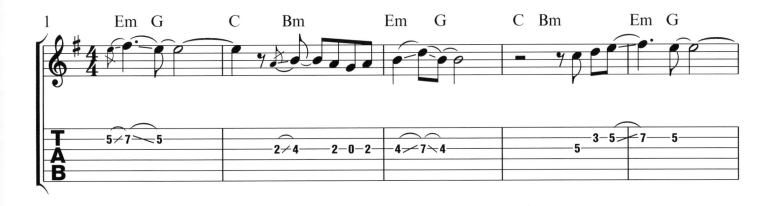

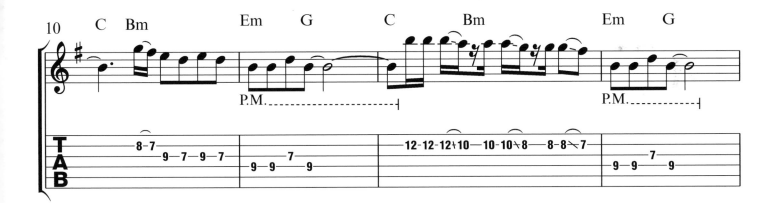

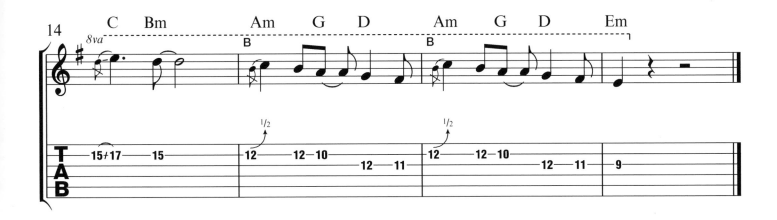

▶▶ SLASH

"Vibrato is basically a moving bend, but not going so far. The hand sits the same way but the physical action is different. The technique is about conveying emotions."

For the second solo over this backing we'll take a more aggressive approach.

The solo starts with a unison bend at the 12th fret, followed by a long, tumbling E natural minor scale that turns back on itself several times before coming to rest. There's then a dramatic move to the open position with an open bottom E and a classic pentatonic minor bend on the 3rd string. Bar 7 uses double-stops followed by a run on A natural minor for the Am - G - D change.

In bars 9-12 note another example of the use of open strings in conjunction with fretted notes. The top E rings out as the fretted notes descend on the 2nd string, while the open B string sounds as the notes go up the 3rd string. Since both these open strings are prominent notes in the scale of E natural minor it works. Not only that, it pleases the ear as an example of 'contrary motion' – as the notes climb in bars 10 and 12 the chords are moving downward.

The last two bars use a repeated 'lick' at the 5th and 12th frets, with a slight twist (the use of F♯ instead of the expected G) – use your first finger to barre the top two strings in both these phrases.

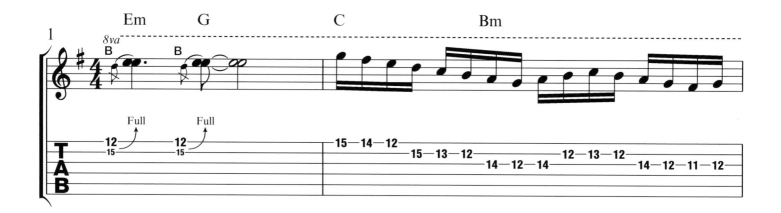

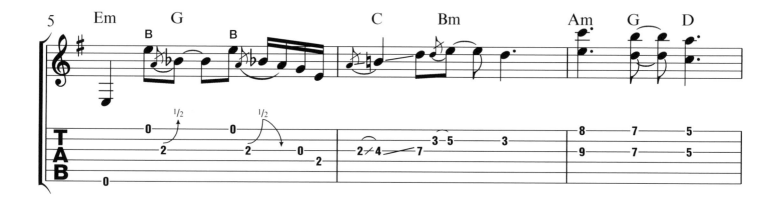

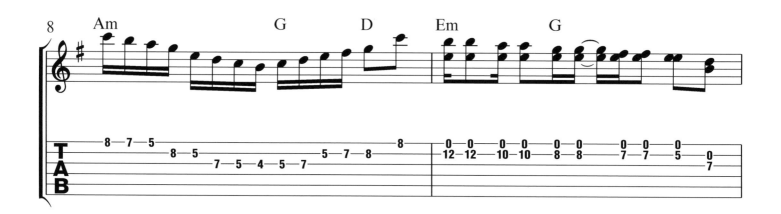

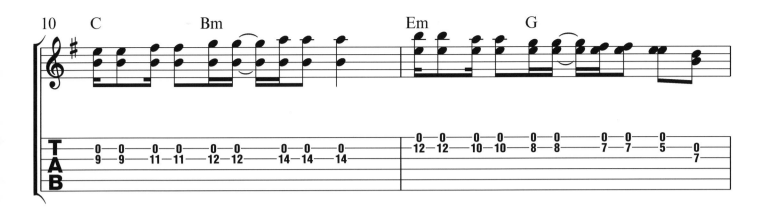

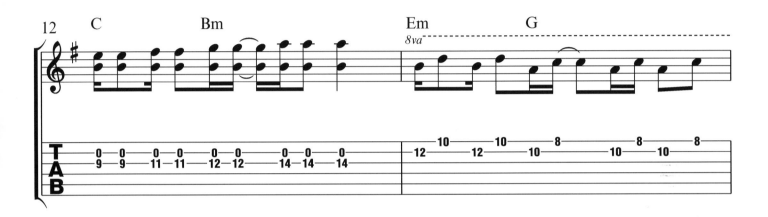

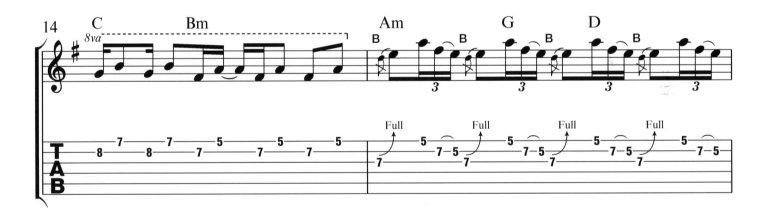

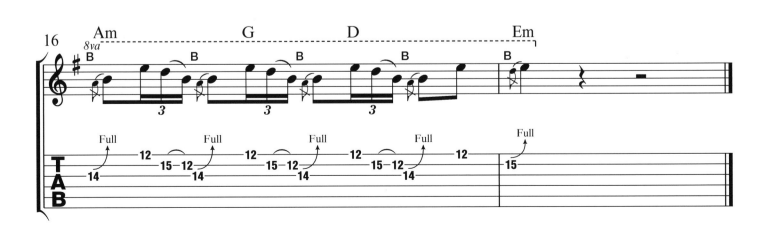

**JIMMY PAGE**

*"It took a long time before I had any sort of dexterity. I used to listen to Ricky Nelson records and pinch James Burton's licks note-for-note."*

# Checklist

Before you play the epic-length last solo, let's just recap on some of the points you've learned about how to solo. Next time you try to work on a solo, check this list and see if your solo meets these requirements. First, let's check over some of the the raw materials out of which a lead break can be made:

# Resources

1. Select the right scale for the key. For minor keys use the pentatonic minor and the natural minor. For major keys use the pentatonic major and the major scale itself. For a blues / hard-rock feel, try the pentatonic minor in a major key.

2. You can stay on the same scale for a whole sequence, but remember to watch out for any chords that are not in key. These will need some adjustments. You may also choose a different scale to match some of the individual chords in a progression.

3. Don't forget arpeggios – lead solos don't just have to consist of scales – try playing within a chord shape.

4. You can combine open strings and fretted notes where they fit in with the backing – for example, use the top two strings over a backing of E major.

5. Use double-stops for contrast, and to emphasise the tonality of a sequence.

6. Bends will allow you to use more notes without shifting position. You can use unison bends to emphasise notes.

7. Sound-effects: distortion, fuzz, compression, phasing, chorus, delay and wah-wah are the most popular for solos. If your guitar has a tremolo arm, that can be used to create a variety of musical effects. Don't forget about changing pick-ups too!

*"I use coins instead of a plectrum because they're not flexible. I think you get more control if all the flexing is due to the movement in your fingers."*

# Composition

Some important musical points to remember
when you're trying to put together a solo:

1. Melody. Can you whistle or sing parts of the
solo?

2. Length. Judge how long the solo should be in
relation to the rest of the song.

3. Phrasing makes the difference between a good
solo and a collection of disconnected scales. Use
repetition, question and answer ideas, contrast
scale movement with leaps, play at different
octaves, or use contrary motion.

4. Rhythm. Try and lock in with the rhythm of
the backing. Play everything with rhythmic
conviction.

5. Mood. Make sure the solo is appropriate for
the mood of the music.

▶▶ **ERIC CLAPTON**
*"There's always someone faster, isn't there? It's best to just try and play well.
Not necessarily brilliant."*

# 'And Shall We Find The Way'

Now you have the opportunity to solo at length over 40 bars!

This chord sequence is in E minor and doesn't use any unusual chords, so the E natural minor and E pentatonic minor scales will work perfectly. The 8-bar sequence occurs five times.

This lead break uses many of the techniques mentioned in this book. Although none of the individual phrases are difficult, you will have to practise before you will be able to put it all together. We can break down the solo as follows:

**Bars 1-8:** Introduction. The first time through, the rhythm section is subdued and you'll notice the guitar is reserved here, using an arpeggio idea in bars 1 and 5 and climbing slowly up the E natural minor scale from C in bar 3. Notice how the ascending notes in bars 7-8 create a sense of drama.

**Bars 9-16:** With the full entry of the drums the track lifts off. The guitar plays a strongly defined melodic phrase centred on the note B at the 7th fret – each time the phrase is repeated, it has a slightly different ending. In bar 15 the phrasing echoes the 'climb' in bars 7-8.

**Bars 17-24:** Bars 17-20 are occupied by a melody which uses a highly syncopated rhythm which stretches across the beats, creating a 'floating' feel. Notice the shock of the high E in bar 17. To off-set the sweetness of this phrase, you'll hear the 'dirty' semitone bend at the end of bar 20, using a blues note. Bars 21-22 are based on an idea that uses the open B string to support a scale figure going up the top string, producing a full sound. Bar 23 repeats bar 15, and echoes bars 7-8. Then bar 24 leads us into the next section with a rapid ascending scale of E natural minor. Make sure you get the fingering right! Refer back to the natural minor scale which starts on the 5th string in Section 2 if necessary.

**Bars 25-32:** The intensity increases with a repeated semitone hammer-on / pull-off figure. The figure in bar 25 is the same as that in bar 27 but it sounds different. Why? Because the chord over which you're playing has changed. In bar 29 a dancing triplet figure is introduced, which leads into the figure in bar 32 (best remembered by relating it to an ordinary D chord shape).

**Bars 33-40:** The final stretch starts with a 'raked' E minor triad at the 12th fret. The 'rake' technique involves hitting the strings fractionally one after the other with a single sweep of the pick, instead of playing them all at once. The high bend in bar 35 leads down to the double-stops in bar 37. There's a final burst of E pentatonic minor notes in bar 39, before the solo concludes on the E natural minor scale in bars 39-40.

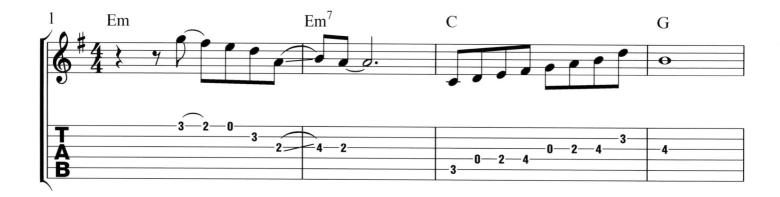

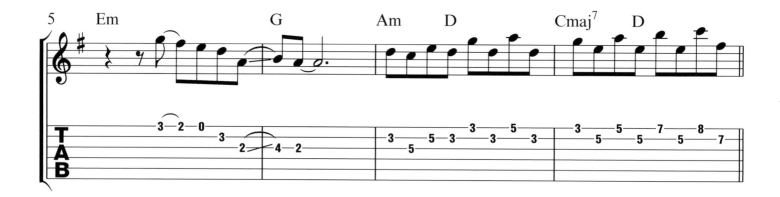

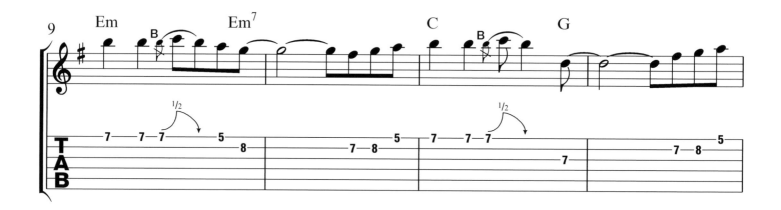

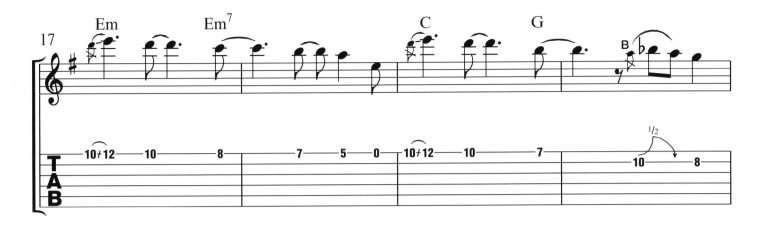

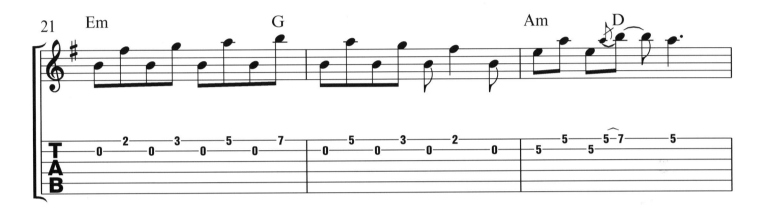

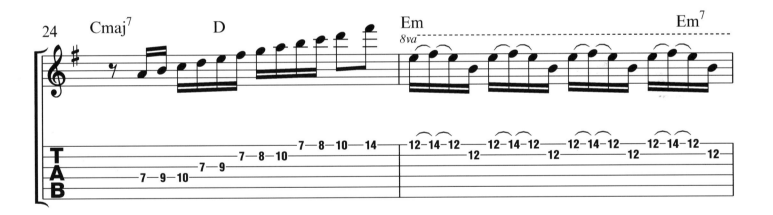

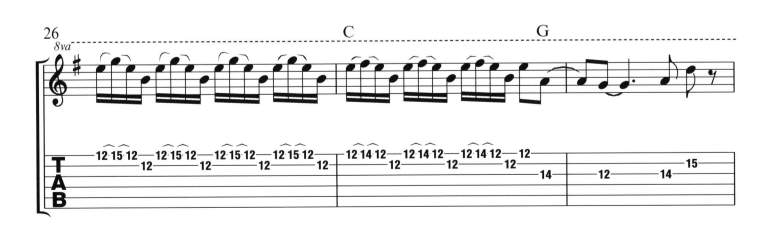

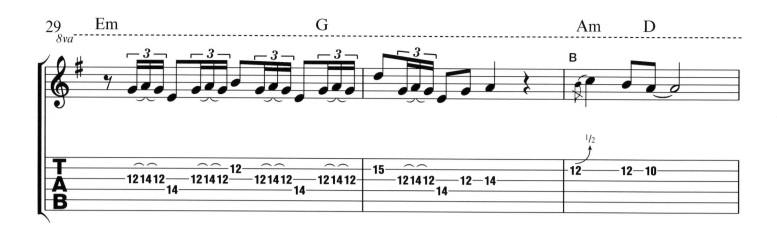

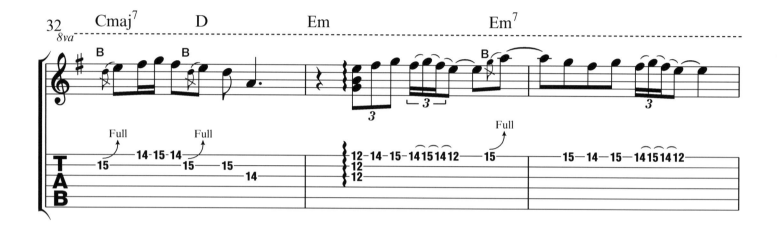

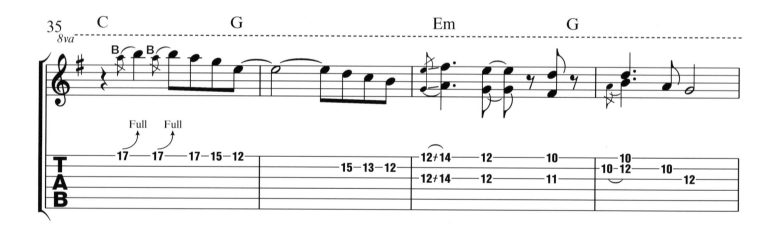

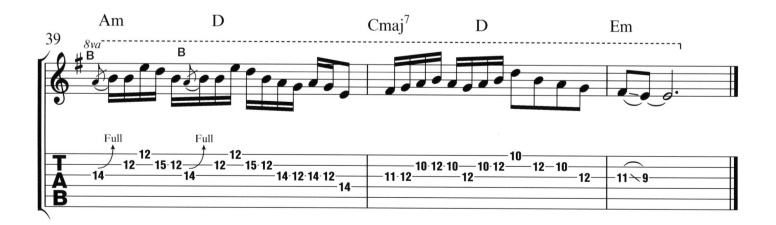

# Where Now?

If you've mastered the exercises and solos in this book you'll now have all the techniques and tricks you need to be able to play authentic lead guitar solos. If you want to know more, try some of the other titles in the ▶▶Fast*Forward* series, or explore some of the other music books available:

Power Blues Guitar Solos (Book + CD)
AM91062

Go Solo Rock Guitar (Book + CD)
AM91416

Great Rock Solos for Guitar Tab
AM92397

In Deep With Jimi Hendrix
AM929445

Lead Guitar
AM11198

Learn To Play Rock Chord Riffs (Book + CD)
AM90237

Metal Lead Guitar Method 1 (Book + CD)
HLE00699321

Metal Lead Guitar Method 2 (Book + CD)
HLE00699322

Play Guitar Like Richie Sambora
AM79815

Carlos Santana for Guitar Tab
AM92348

Blur for Easy Guitar Tab
AM936859

Play Guitar With Blur (Book + CD)
AM935320

Bon Jovi for Easy Guitar Tab
AM9368760

Eric Clapton for Guitar Tab
AM92131

Jimi Hendrix Solos: Guitar School
AM91388

John Lee Hooker for Guitar Tab
AM91516

Official Mark Knopfler Guitar Styles 1
DG70600

Official Mark Knopfler Guitar Styles 2
DG70618

John Martyn for Guitar Tab
AM91531

Steve Miller for Guitar Tab
AM933163

Play Guitar With Oasis (Book + CD)
AM935330

Play Guitar With Pulp (Book + CD)
AM938124

Play Guitar With Rolling Stones (Book + CD)
AM90247

Stevie Ray Vaughan for Guitar Tab
AM929291

Play Guitar With Paul Weller (Book + CD)
AM937827

Paul Weller for Guitar Tab
AM935847

# Guitar Tablature Explained

**Guitar music can be notated three different ways: on a musical stave, in tablature, and in rhythm slashes**

**RHYTHM SLASHES** are written above the stave. Strum chords in the rhythm indicated. Round noteheads indicate single notes.

**THE MUSICAL STAVE** shows pitches and rhythms and is divided by lines into bars. Pitches are named after the first seven letters of the alphabet.

**TABLATURE** graphically represents the guitar fingerboard. Each horizontal line represents a string, and each number represents a fret.

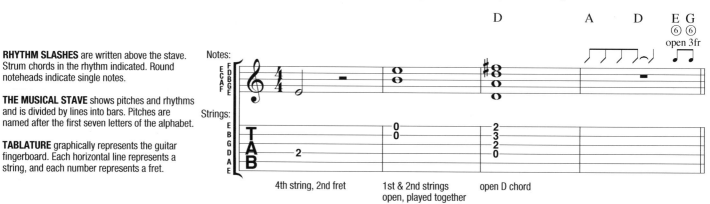

4th string, 2nd fret     1st & 2nd strings open, played together     open D chord

# definitions for special guitar notation

**SEMI-TONE BEND:** Strike the note and bend up a semi-tone (1/2 step).

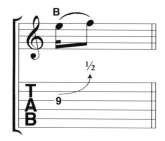

**WHOLE-TONE BEND:** Strike the note and bend up a whole-tone (whole step).

**GRACE NOTE BEND:** Strike the note and bend as indicated. Play the first note as quickly as possible.

**QUARTER-TONE BEND:** Strike the note and bend up a 1/4 step.

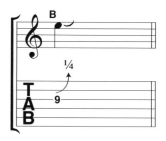

**BEND & RELEASE:** Strike the note and bend up as indicated, then release back to the original note.

**BEND & RESTRIKE:** Strike the note and bend as indicated then restrike the string where the symbol occurs.

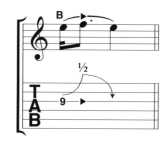

**PRE-BEND:** Bend the note as indicated, then strike it.

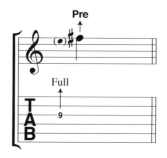

**PRE-BEND & RELEASE:** Bend the note as indicated. Strike it and release the note back to the original pitch.

**HAMMER-ON:** Strike the first (lower) note with one finger, then sound the higher note (on the same string) with another finger by fretting it without picking.

**PULL-OFF:** Place both fingers on the notes to be sounded, Strike the first note and without picking, pull the finger off to sound the second (lower) note.

**LEGATO SLIDE (GLISS):** Strike the first note and then slide the same fret-hand finger up or down to the second note. The second note is not struck.

**SHIFT SLIDE (GLISS & RESTRIKE):** Same as legato slide, except the second note is struck.

**NATURAL HARMONIC:** Strike the note while the fret-hand lightly touches the string directly over the fret indicated.

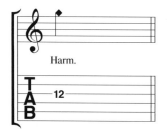

**PICK SCRAPE:** The edge of the pick is rubbed down (or up) the string, producing a scratchy sound.

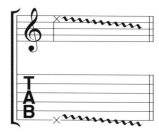

**PALM MUTING:** The note is partially muted by the pick hand lightly touching the string(s) just before the bridge.

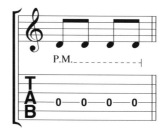

**MUFFLED STRINGS:** A percussive sound is produced by laying the fret hand across the string(s) without depressing, and striking them with the pick hand.

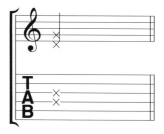

**NOTE:** The speed of any bend is indicated by the music notation and tempo.

# ▶▶ *FastForward*™
# Guide To Guitar

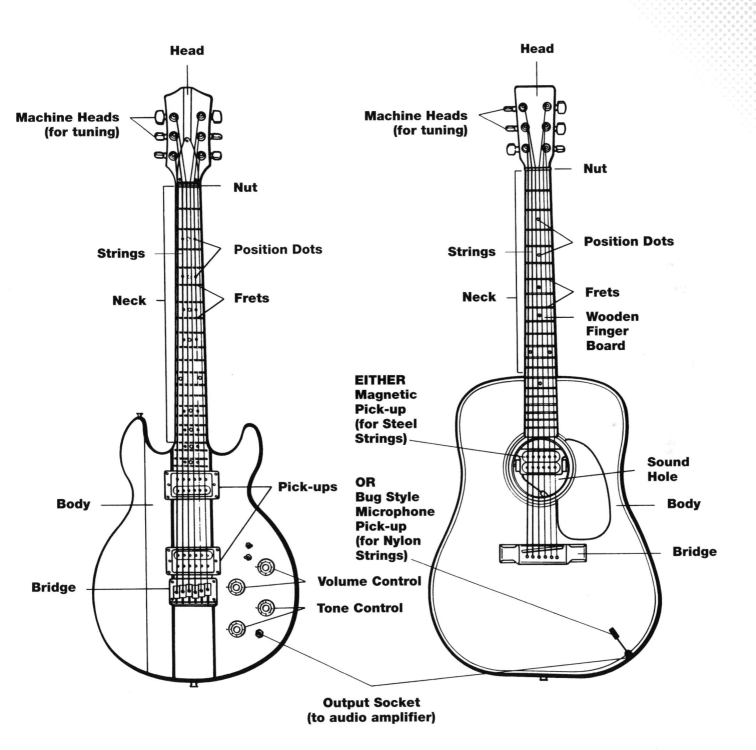

**Head**

**Machine Heads (for tuning)**

**Nut**

**Strings**

**Position Dots**

**Neck**

**Frets**

**Pick-ups**

**Body**

**Bridge**

**Head**

**Machine Heads (for tuning)**

**Nut**

**Strings**

**Position Dots**

**Neck**

**Frets**

**Wooden Finger Board**

**EITHER Magnetic Pick-up (for Steel Strings)**

**OR Bug Style Microphone Pick-up (for Nylon Strings)**

**Volume Control**

**Tone Control**

**Sound Hole**

**Body**

**Bridge**

**Output Socket (to audio amplifier)**

## The Guitar

Whether you have an acoustic or an electric guitar, the principles of playing are fundamentally the same, and so are most of the features on both instruments.

In order to 'electrify' an acoustic guitar (as in the diagram), a magnetic pick up can be attached to those guitars with steel strings or a 'bug' style microphone pick-up can be attached to guitars with nylon strings.

If in doubt check with your local music shop.

# Tuning Your Guitar

### Tuning
Accurate tuning of the guitar is essential, and is achieved by winding the machine heads up or down. It is always better to 'tune up' to the correct pitch rather than down.

Therefore, if you find that the pitch of your string is higher (sharper) than the correct pitch, you should 'wind down' below the correct pitch, and then 'tune up' to it.

### Relative Tuning
Tuning the guitar to itself without the aid of a pitch pipe or other tuning device.

### Other Methods Of Tuning
Pitch pipe
Tuning fork
Dedicated electronic guitar tuner

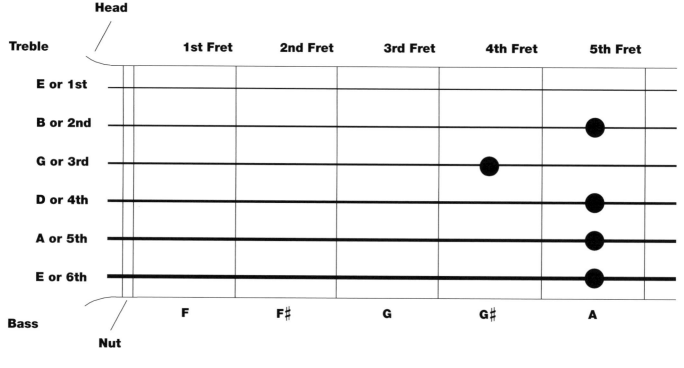

 Press down where indicated, one at a time, following the instructions below.

Estimate the pitch of the 6th string as near as possible to **E** or at least a comfortable pitch (not too high or you might break other strings in tuning up).

Then, while checking the various positions on the above diagram, place a finger from your left hand on:

The 5th fret of the E or 6th string and **tune the open A** (or 5th string) to the note (A)

The 5th fret of the A or 5th string and **tune the open D** (or 4th string) to the note (D)

The 5th fret of the D or 4th string and **tune the open G** (or 3rd string) to the note (G)

The 4th fret of the G or 3rd string and **tune the open B** (or 2nd string) to the note (B)

The 5th fret of the B or 2nd string and **tune the open E** (or 1st string) to the note (E)

# Chord Boxes

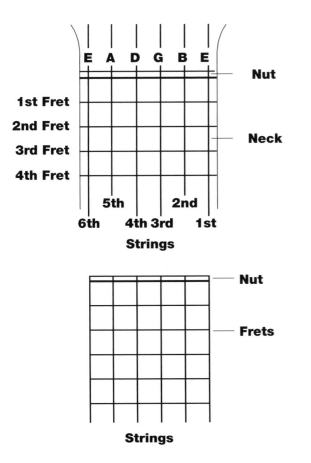

E A D G B E

Nut

1st Fret

2nd Fret

Neck

3rd Fret

4th Fret

5th    2nd

6th   4th 3rd   1st

**Strings**

Nut

Frets

**Strings**

**The A Chord**

6 5 4 3 2 1

Frets

1st

**1** **2** **3**   2nd

3rd

4th

5th

x

**x** = do not play this string

All chords are major chords unless otherwise indicated.

### Left Hand
Place all three fingers into position and press down firmly. Keep your thumb around the middle of the back of the neck and directly behind your 1st and 2nd fingers.

### Right Hand Thumb Or Plectrum
Slowly play each string, starting with the 5th or A string and moving up to the 1st or E string.

*If there is any buzzing, perhaps you need to:-*
Position your fingers nearer the metal fret (towards you); or adjust the angle of your hand; or check that the buzz is not elsewhere on the guitar by playing the open strings in the same manner.

*Finally*, your nails may be too long, in which case you are pressing down at an extreme angle and therefore not firmly enough. Also the pad of one of your fingers may be in the way of the next string for the same reason.

So, cut your nails to a more comfortable length and then try to keep them as near vertical to the fretboard as possible.

Once you have a 'buzz-free' sound, play the chord a few times and then remove your fingers and repeat the exercise until your positioning is right instinctively.

Chord boxes are diagrams of the guitar neck viewed head upwards, face on, as illustrated in the above drawings. The horizontal double line at the top is the nut, the other horizontal lines are the frets. The vertical lines are the strings starting from E or 6th on the left to E or 1st on the right.

Any dots with numbers inside them simply indicate which finger goes where. Any strings marked with an **x** must not be played.

The fingers of your hand are numbered 1, 2, 3, & 4 as in the diagram below.

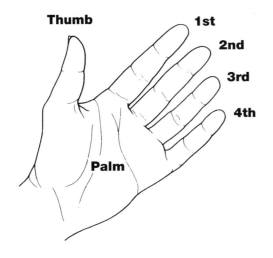

Thumb     1st

2nd

3rd

4th

Palm

# Holding The Guitar

Keep your thumb slightly to the left of your fingers which should be above the three treble strings as shown.

The picture above shows a comfortable position for playing rock or pop guitar

### The Right Hand
When STRUMMING (brushing your fingers across the strings), hold your fingers together.

### The Plectrum
Many modern guitar players prefer to use a plectrum to strike the strings. Plectrums come in many sizes, shapes and thicknesses and are available from your local music shop.

Start with a fairly large, soft one if possible, with a grip. The photo shows the correct way to hold your plectrum.

When PICKING (plucking strings individually), hold your wrist further away from the strings than for strumming.

### The Left Hand
Use your fingertips to press down on the strings in the positions described. Your thumb should be behind your 1st and 2nd fingers pressing on the middle of the back of the neck.